BONUS!

LOOK FOR THE CAMERA in our instructions and watch our technique videos made just for you! **www.LeisureArts.com/75537**

Two-Hour Neckwear

Chunky yarn, big needles, and a couple of hours are all you need to knit one of these fabulous cowls. They're great for gifts or for adding a quick change to your wardrobe. Choose from patterns for Beginner to Intermediate skill levels.

LEISURE ARTS, INC.
Maumelle, Arkansas

Bow Cowl

BEGINNER

Finished Size: 7½" wide x 24" circumference (19 cm x 61 cm)

SHOPPING LIST

Yarn (Jumbo Weight) JUMBO 7

[10.5 ounces, 64 yards

(300 grams, 58 meters) per skein**]**:

- ☐ 2 skeins

Knitting Needles

Straight,

- ☐ Size 19 (15 mm)
  or size needed for gauge

Hold two strands of yarn together throughout.

GAUGE INFORMATION

In Seed Stitch,

7 sts = 7½" (19 cm)

4 rows = 3" (7.5 cm)

TECHNIQUE USED

E-Wrap Cast On *(Fig. 1, page 42)*

INSTRUCTIONS

Cast on 7 sts.

Rows 1-38: K1, (P1, K1) across.

Row 39: K1, P1, bind off next 3 sts, K1.

Row 40: K1, P1, e-wrap cast on 3 sts, P1, K1.

Rows 41-46: K1, (P1, K1) across.

Bind off all sts in pattern.

Finishing

To form the Bow, insert cast on end through opening on Row 39 for approximately 4" (10 cm).

To form the knot of the Bow, wrap two strands of yarn around the middle of the Bow 10-12 times **or** to desired thickness; secure ends at back of Bow.

Fringe Pocket Cowl

Shown on page 7.

BEGINNER

Finished Pocket Size: 7¼" wide x 12½" circumference (18.5 cm x 32 cm)

SHOPPING LIST

Yarn (Bulky Weight) BULKY 5

[3.5 ounces, 78 yards (100 grams, 71 meters) per skein]:

☐ 2 skeins

Knitting Needles

Straight,

☐ Size 17 (12.75 mm) **or** size needed for gauge

Additional Supplies

☐ Crochet hook, size K (6.5 mm) or larger (for fringe)

Hold two strands of yarn together throughout.

GAUGE INFORMATION

In Seed Stitch,

13 sts = 7¼" (18.5 cm)

INSTRUCTIONS

Cast on 13 sts.

Row 1: K1, (P1, K1) across.

Repeat Row 1 for Seed St pattern until piece measures approximately 12½" (32 cm) from cast on edge.

Bind off all sts in pattern.

Finishing

Cut 26, 70" (178 cm) long strands of yarn for fringe.

Fold piece in half, matching sts of cast on and bind off edges together.

Using a crochet hook, holding two strands of yarn together for each fringe, and inserting hook through **both** layers, add fringe across ***(Figs. 7a & b, page 46)***; creating a pocket for the fringe.

Lay piece flat on a hard surface and trim the ends.

Dramatic Pom-Pom Cowl

EASY

Finished Size: Approximately 75" (190.5 cm) circumference

SHOPPING LIST

Yarn (Super Bulky Weight) SUPER BULKY 6

[4 ounces, 64 yards
(113 grams, 59 meters) per skein]:

- ☐ Pink - 1 skein

[5 ounces, 81 yards
(142 grams, 74 meters) per skein]:

- ☐ Blue - 1 skein
- ☐ Orange - 1 skein
- ☐ Purple - 1 skein
- ☐ Green - 1 skein

Additional Supplies

- ☐ 3" (7.5 cm) square Cardboard **or** 3" (7.5 cm) Pom-pom maker

INSTRUCTIONS

Make five 3" (7.5 cm) pom-poms of **each** color *(Figs. 6a-c, page 45)*.

Tie the pom-poms together using tails; then hide the tails into each pom-pom and trim.

Fair Isle Cowl

INTERMEDIATE

Finished Size: 7" wide x 36" circumference
(18 cm x 91.5 cm)

SHOPPING LIST

Yarn (Super Bulky Weight) SUPER BULKY 6
[6 ounces, 121 yards
(170 grams, 110 meters) per skein]:

- ☐ Orange - 1 skein
- ☐ Cream - 1 skein

Knitting Needle
36" (91.5 cm) Circular,

- ☐ Size 17 (12.75 mm)
  or size needed for gauge

Additional Supplies

- ☐ Marker

GAUGE INFORMATION

In Stockinette Stitch
(knit each round),
8 sts = 4" (10 cm)
8 rnds = 3" (7.5 cm)

INSTRUCTIONS

With Orange and using circular needle, cast on 72 sts, place marker to mark beginning of the round ***(see Using a Circular Needle, page 42 and Markers, page 41)***.

Rnd 1: Purl around.

Rnd 2: Knit around.

Rnd 3: Purl around.

Rnds 4-7: Knit around.

Rnds 8-14: Follow Chart.

Rnds 15-17: Knit around.

Rnd 18: Purl around.

Rnd 19: Knit around.

Rnd 20: Purl around.

Bind off all sts in **knit**.

FOLLOWING A CHART

Designs for Fair Isle knitting are worked from a chart. It is easier to follow a chart than written instructions and you can also see what the pattern looks like. The chart shows each stitch as a square indicating what color each stitch should be. Visualize the chart as your fabric, beginning at the bottom edge.

Always follow the chart from **right** to **left**. For ease in following the chart, place a ruler above the round being worked to help keep your place.

When changing colors, always pick up the new color yarn from **beneath** the dropped yarn and keep the color which has just been worked to the left ***(Fig. A)***. This will prevent holes in the finished piece. Take extra care to keep your tension even.

Fig. A

CHART

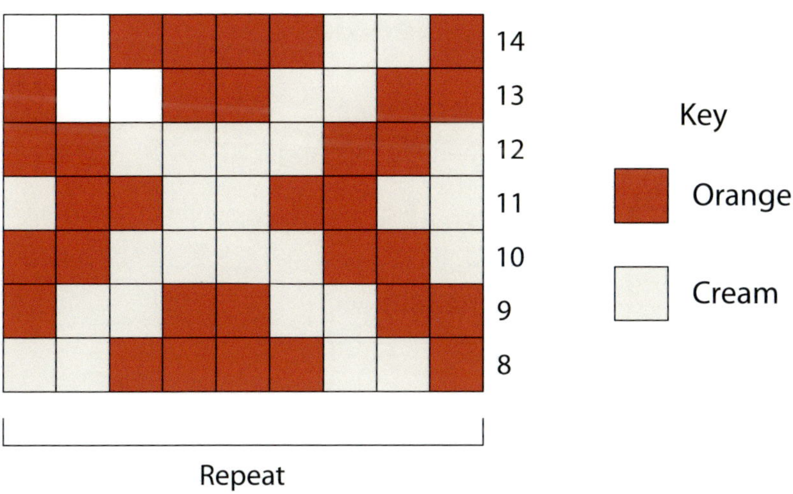

Garter Flap Cowl

EASY

Finished Size: 5½" wide x 20" circumference
(14 cm x 51 cm)

SHOPPING LIST

Yarn (Super Bulky Weight) SUPER BULKY 6
[5 ounces, 156 yards
(142 grams, 143 meters) per skein**]**:
- ☐ 1 skein

Knitting Needles
Straight,
- ☐ Size 17 (12.75 mm)
  or size needed for gauge

Additional Supplies
- ☐ Yarn needle
- ☐ 2" (50 mm) Button

Hold two strands of yarn together throughout.

GAUGE INFORMATION

In Garter Stitch (knit each row),
10 sts = 5½" (14 cm);
11 rows = 4" (10 cm)

TECHNIQUE USED

SSK *(Figs. 4a-c, page 44)*

INSTRUCTIONS

Cast on 18 sts.

Rows 1-4: Knit across.

Flap Shaping

Row 1 (Decrease row)**:** K1, SSK, knit across: 17 sts.

Row 2 (Right side)**:** Knit across.

Rows 3-16: Repeat Rows 1 and 2, 7 times: 10 sts.

Knit every row until piece measures approximately 20" (51 cm) from cast on edge, ending by working a **wrong** side row.

Bind Off/Joining Row

Fold piece in half with cast on edge **behind** sts on last row. Matching sts, insert needle through next st on left needle **and** through cast on st, knitting them together as one st *(Fig. A)*. Knit next st on left needle with next cast on st; then bind off first st on right needle. Continue across, leaving last 8 cast on sts unjoined.

Fig. A

Using photo as a guide for placement, fold Flap to **right** side, then sew on button through both layers.

Garter Fringe Cowl

Shown on pages 18 & 19.

BEGINNER

Finished Size: 8" wide (at widest area) x 20"circumference (20.5 cm x 51 cm)

SHOPPING LIST

Yarn (Medium Weight) MEDIUM 4

Version A

[7 ounces, 364 yards
(198 grams, 333 meters) per skein]:

- ☐ Green - 1 skein

[5 ounces, 236 yards
(141 grams, 215 meters) per skein]:

- ☐ Variegated - 1 skein

Version B

[7 ounces, 370 yards
(198 grams, 338 meters) per skein]:

- ☐ Black - 1 skein
- ☐ Maroon - 1 skein

Knitting Needles

Straight,

- ☐ Size 19 (15 mm) **or** size needed for gauge

Additional Supplies

- ☐ Crochet hook, size K (6.5 mm) **or** larger (for fringe)

Hold four strands of yarn (2 strands of **each** color) together throughout.

GAUGE INFORMATION

In Garter Stitch (knit each row),
6 sts = 4" (10 cm)
10 rows = 3" (7.5 cm)

INSTRUCTIONS

Cast on 12 sts.

Knit each row until piece measures approximately 13" (33 cm) from cast on edge.

Next Row: (K1, P1) across.

Repeat last row for K1, P1 ribbing until piece measures approximately 20" (51 cm) from cast on edge.

Bind off all sts in ribbing.

Finishing

Cut 48, 12" (30.5 cm) long strands of yarn for fringe, 24 of **each** color of yarn.

Fold Cowl in half, matching sts of cast on and bind off edges together.

Using a crochet hook, holding two strands of **each** color yarn (4 strands total) together for each fringe, and inserting hook through **both** layers, add fringe across ***(Figs. 7a & b, page 46)***.

Lay piece flat on a hard surface and trim the ends.

Herringbone Cowl

INTERMEDIATE

Finished Size: 5¼" wide x 20" circumference
(13.25 cm x 51 cm)

SHOPPING LIST

Yarn (Super Bulky Weight) SUPER BULKY 6

[5 ounces, 81 yards
(142 grams, 74 meters) per skein]:

☐ 1 skein

Knitting Needles

Straight,

☐ Size 17 (12.75 mm)
or size needed for gauge

Additional Supplies

☐ 5/8" (16 mm) wide Ribbon - 36" (91.5 cm)

GAUGE INFORMATION

In pattern,

16 sts = 5¼" (13.25 cm)

9 rows = 4" (10 cm)

TECHNIQUES USED

YO *(Fig. A)*

Fig. A

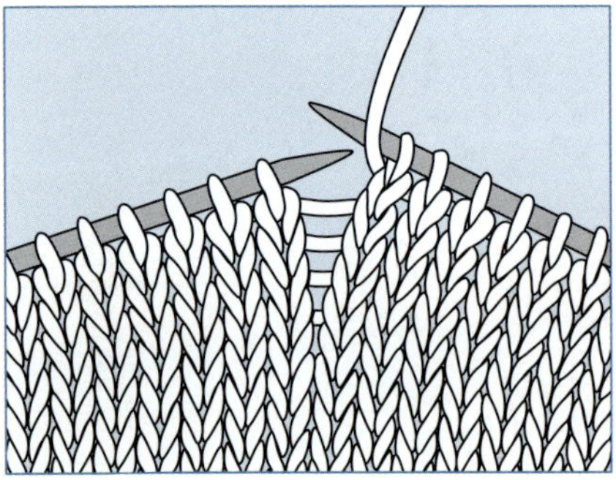

Slip 1 as if to **knit**, K1, YO, pass slipped st over 2 sts ***(Fig. B)***

Fig. B

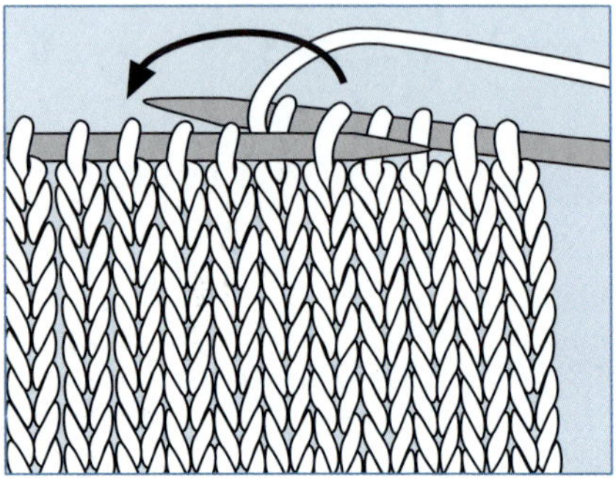

P2 tog ***(Fig. 5, page 44)***

INSTRUCTIONS

Cast on 16 sts.

Row 1 (Right side)**:** K1, ★ slip 1 as if to **knit**, K1, YO, pass slipped st over 2 sts; repeat from ★ across, K1.

Row 2: ★ P2 tog but do **not** drop old sts off needle, purl first st on left needle *(Fig. C)*, drop both sts off left needle; repeat from ★ across.

Fig. C

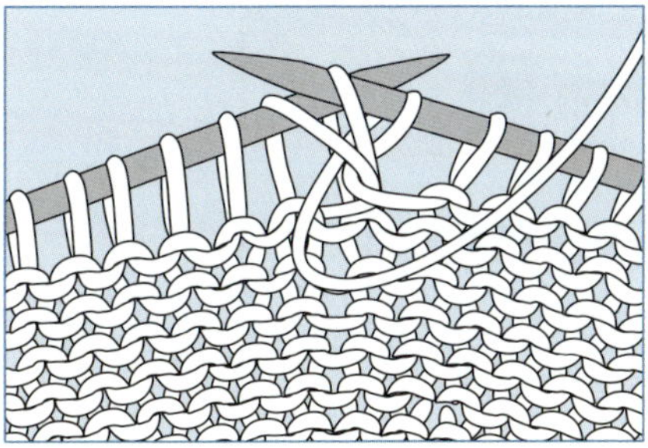

Repeat Rows 1 and 2 for pattern until piece measures approximately 20" (51 cm) from cast on edge, ending by working a **right** side row.

Bind off all sts in **purl**.

Finishing

With **right** side facing, place cast on and bind off edges together. Thread ribbon through first stitch on each side, then going from side-to-side, lace ribbon through each stitch to opposite end; tie ribbon in a bow.

Loop Stitch Cowl

EASY

Finished Size: 13¼" wide x 24" circumference (33.5 cm x 61 cm)

SHOPPING LIST

Yarn (Super Bulky Weight) SUPER BULKY 6

[4 ounces, 80 yards
(113 grams, 73 meters) per skein]:

- ☐ 2 skeins

Knitting Needles

Straight,

- ☐ Size 13 (9 mm)
  or size needed for gauge

Additional Supplies

- ☐ Yarn needle

GAUGE INFORMATION

In Loop Stitch,

6 sts = 3½" (9 cm)

8 rows = 4" (10 cm)

STITCH GUIDE

LOOP STITCH

Knit next st, do **not** drop old st from left needle *(Fig. A)*, pull loop of st just made to approximately 3" (7.5 cm) long. Remove right needle from st and knit through back loop of same st *(Fig. B)*, allowing the st to drop from left needle.

Fig. A

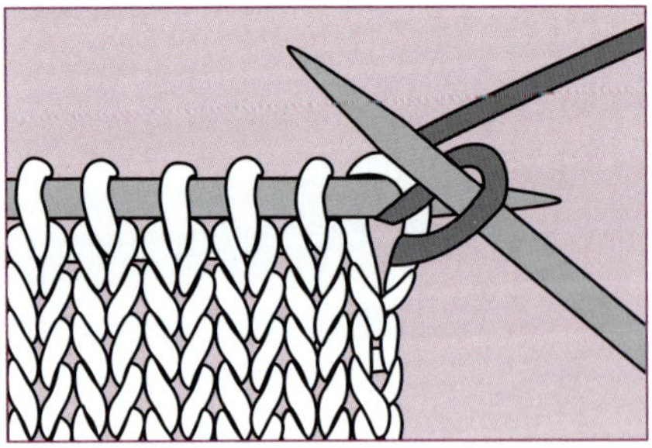

Fig. B

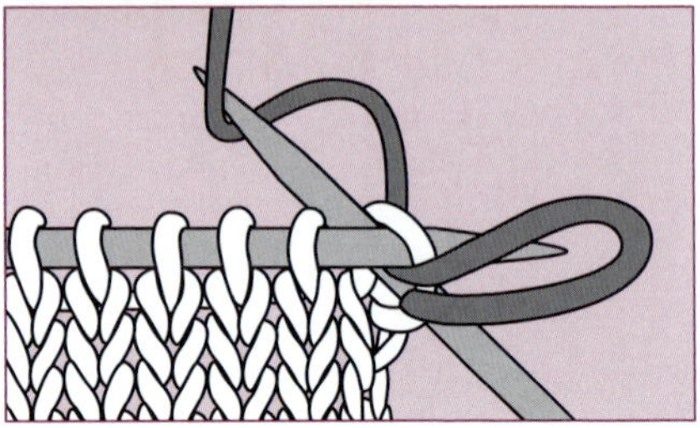

INSTRUCTIONS

Cast on 23 sts.

Row 1: Knit across.

Row 2 (Right side)**:** Work Loop Stitch across.

Rows 3 and 4: Knit across.

Repeat Rows 1-4 for pattern until piece measures approximately 24" (61 cm) from cast on edge, ending by working Row 3.

Bind off all sts in **knit**, leaving a long end for sewing.

With **right** side of piece together, sew cast on and bind off edges together.

Pom-Pom Closure Cowl

Shown on page 29.

INTERMEDIATE

Finished Size: 5" wide x 23" long (12.5 x 58.5 cm) (excluding pom-pom)

SHOPPING LIST

Yarn (Medium Weight) MEDIUM 4

[3.5 ounces, 151 yards (100 grams, 138 meters) per skein]:

- ☐ 4 skeins

Knitting Needles

Double pointed (set of 4),

- ☐ Size 17 (12.75 mm) **or** size needed for gauge

Additional Supplies

- ☐ Split-ring marker
- ☐ Yarn needle
- ☐ 3" (7.5 cm) square Cardboard **or** 3" (7.5 cm) Pom-pom maker

Hold four strands of yarn together throughout.

GAUGE INFORMATION

In Stockinette Stitch
(knit each rnd),
6 sts and 8 rnds = 3" (7.5 cm)

TECHNIQUE USED

E-Wrap Cast On *(Fig. 1, page 42)*

INSTRUCTIONS

With double pointed needles, cast on 20 sts; place a split-ring marker around first st to mark the beginning of the round *(see Using Double Pointed Needles, page 43 and Markers, page 41)*.

Knit each rnd until piece measures 21" (53.5 cm) from cast on edge.

Pom-Pom Opening

Rnd 1: K4, bind off next 3 sts, K 12: 17 sts.

Rnd 2: K4, e-wrap cast on 3 sts, K 13: 20 sts.

Rnds 3-5: Knit around.

Bind off all sts in **knit**.

Finishing

Make one 4" (10 cm) pom-pom *(Figs. 6a-c, page 45)*.

Sew pom-pom to the cast on edge of piece.

Use pom-pom to connect Cowl by pushing it through opening.

Multidirectional Cowl

EASY +

Finished Size: 9" wide x 21" circumference (23 cm x 53.5 cm)

SHOPPING LIST

Yarn (Bulky Weight) BULKY 5

[3.5 ounces, 120 yards
(100 grams, 109 meters) per skein]:

- ☐ Red - 1 skein

(Medium Weight) MEDIUM 4

[3.5 ounces, 270 yards
(100 grams, 247 meters) per skein]:

- ☐ Variegated - 2 skeins

Knitting Needles

Straight,

- ☐ Size 13 (9 mm) **and**
- ☐ Size 17 (12.75 mm)
  or sizes needed for gauge

Additional Supplies

- ☐ Yarn needle

Hold three strands of yarn (2 strands of Variegated **and** one strand of Red) together throughout.

GAUGE INFORMATION

With larger size needles,
in Stockinette Stitch
(knit one row, purl one row),
6 sts = 4" (10 cm)
8 rows = 3" (7.5 cm)

INSTRUCTIONS

First Section

With larger size needles, cast on 14 sts.

Beginning with a **purl** row, work in Stockinette Stitch for approximately 9" (23 cm), ending by working a **purl** row.

Bind off all sts in **knit**, do **not** cut yarn, slip last st onto smaller size needle.

Second Section

With **knit** side of First Section facing and using smaller size needle, pick up 19 sts evenly spaced across ends of rows *(Fig. A)*: 20 sts.

Fig. A

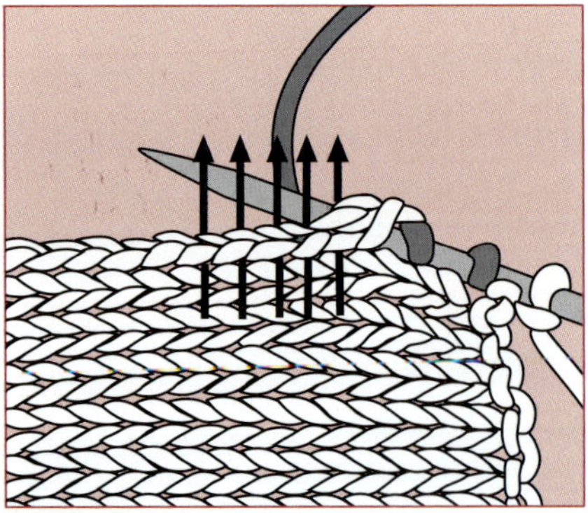

Beginning with a **knit** row, work in Reverse Stockinette Stitch (knit one row, purl one row) until Second Section measures 9" (23 cm) , ending by working a **purl** row.

Third Section

Beginning with a **purl** row, work in Stockinette Stitch until Third Section measures approximately 3" (7.5 cm), ending by working a **knit** row.

Bind off all sts in **purl**, leaving a long end for sewing.

With **knit** sides of First and Third Sections together, sew bind off edge of Third Section to ends of rows on First Section.

DIAGRAM

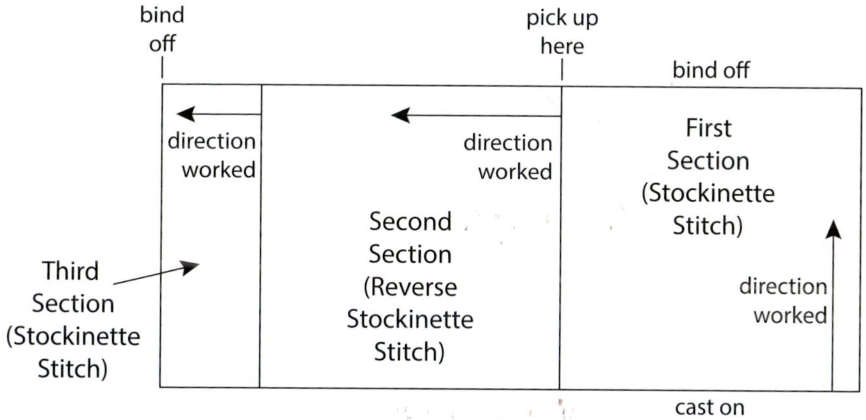

Side Buttoned Cowl

EASY

Finished Size: 8" wide x 27" long
(20.5 cm x 68.5 cm)

SHOPPING LIST

Yarn (Bulky Weight) BULKY 5

[3.5 ounces, 120 yards
(100 grams, 109 meters) per skein]:

- ☐ Teal - 1 skein

[3 ounces, 90 yards
(85 grams, 81 meters) per skein]:

- ☐ Variegated - 2 skeins

Knitting Needles

Straight,

- ☐ Size 13 (9 mm)
  or size needed for gauge

Additional Supplies

- ☐ Yarn needle
- ☐ 2½" (65 mm) Button - 3
- ☐ Magnetic closures - 3

Hold three strands of yarn (2 strands of Variegated **and** one strand of Teal) together throughout.

GAUGE INFORMATION

In Stockinette Stitch
(knit one row, purl one row),
7 sts = 3¾" (9.5 cm)
10 rows = 3" (7.5 cm)

INSTRUCTIONS

Cast on 15 sts.

Row 1 (Right side)**:** (K1, P1) twice, K7, (P1, K1) twice.

Row 2: K1, P1, K1, P9, K1, P1, K1.

Repeat Rows 1 and 2 for pattern until piece measures approximately 25" (63.5 cm) from cast on edge, ending by working Row 2.

Next Row: K1, (P1, K1) across.

Repeat last row until piece measures 27" (68.5 cm) from cast on edge.

Bind off all sts in pattern.

Finishing

With **right** side facing, attach 3 female halves of magnetic snaps evenly spaced to cast on edge of piec. With **wrong** side facing, attach remaining male halves to bottom side edge, spaced to correspond with cast on edge halves.

With **right** side facing, sew buttons over the snaps on side edge.

Striped Cowl

Shown on page 39.

EASY

Finished Size: 9" wide x 24" circumference
(23 cm x 61 cm)

SHOPPING LIST

Yarn (Bulky Weight) BULKY 5
[3.5 ounces, 120 yards
(100 grams, 109 meters) per skein]:
- ☐ Teal - 1 skein
- ☐ Gold - 1 skein

Knitting Needles
Straight,
- ☐ Size 17 (12.75 mm)
  or size needed for gauge

Additional Supplies
- ☐ Yarn needle
- ☐ 3" (7.5 cm) square Cardboard
  or 3" (7.5 cm) Pom-pom maker

GAUGE INFORMATION

In K1, P1 ribbing,
8 sts = 3" (7.5 cm)
6 rows = 2¾" (7 cm)

INSTRUCTIONS

With Teal, cast on 24 sts.

Work in K1, P1 ribbing for approximately 14" (35.5 cm); at end of last row, cut Teal.

With Gold, work 6 rows of K1, P1 ribbing; at end of last row, drop Gold.

With Teal, work 2 rows of K1, P1 ribbing; at end of last row, cut Teal.

Pick up Gold and work 4 rows of K1, P1 ribbing; at end of last row, drop Gold.

With Teal, work 2 rows of K1, P1 ribbing; at end of last row, cut Teal.

Pick up Gold and work 6 rows of K1, P1 ribbing; at end of last row, cut Gold.

With Teal, work 2 rows of K1, P1 ribbing.

Bind off all sts in ribbing, leaving a long end for sewing.

Finishing

Sew bind off and cast on edges together.

Make 4 pom-poms, one solid Teal and one solid Gold, each 3" (7.5 cm), and two 2" (5 cm) Teal/ Gold *(Figs. 6a-c, page 45)*.

Sew pom-poms to the seam.

GENERAL INSTRUCTIONS

ABBREVIATIONS

cm	centimeters
K	knit
mm	millimeters
P	purl
Rnd(s)	Round(s)
SSK	slip, slip, knit
st(s)	stitch(es)
tog	together
YO	yarn over

SYMBOLS & TERMS

★ — work instructions following ★ as many **more** times as indicated in addition to the first time.

( ) or [ ] — work enclosed instructions as **many** times as specified by the number immediately following **or** contains explanatory remarks.

colon (:) — the number(s) given after a colon at the end of a row or round denote(s) the number of stitches you should have on that row or round.

KNITTING NEEDLES																			
U.S.	0	1	2	3	4	5	6	7	8	9	10	10½	11	13	15	17	19	35	50
U.K.	13	12	11	10	9	8	7	6	5	4	3	2	1	00	000	---	---	---	---
Metric - mm	2	2.25	2.75	3.25	3.5	3.75	4	4.5	5	5.5	6	6.5	8	9	10	12.75	15	19	25

BEGINNER	Projects for first-time knitters using basic knit and purl stitches. Minimal shaping.
EASY	Projects using basic stitches, repetitive stitch patterns, simple color changes, and simple shaping and finishing.
INTERMEDIATE	Projects with a variety of stitches, such as basic cables and lace, simple intarsia, double-pointed needles and knitting in the round needle techniques, mid-level shaping and finishing.
EXPERIENCED	Projects using advanced techniques and stitches, such as short rows, fair isle, more intricate intarsia, cables, lace patterns, and numerous color changes.

GAUGE

Exact gauge is **essential** for proper size. Before beginning your Cowl, make a sample swatch in the yarn and needle specified. After completing the swatch, measure it, counting your stitches and rows carefully. If your swatch is larger or smaller than specified, **make another, changing needle size to get the correct gauge**. Keep trying until you find the size needles that will give you the specified gauge.

MARKERS

As a convenience to you, we have used markers to help distinguish the beginning of a round. Place markers as instructed. You may use purchased markers or tie a length of contrasting color yarn around the needle. When you reach a marker on each round, slip it from the left needle to the right needle; remove it when no longer needed.

KNIT TERMINOLOGY		
UNITED STATES		INTERNATIONAL
gauge	=	tension
bind off	=	cast off
yarn over (YO)	=	yarn forward (yfwd) **or** yarn around needle (yrn)

Yarn Weight Symbol & Names	LACE 0	SUPER FINE 1	FINE 2	LIGHT 3	MEDIUM 4	BULKY 5	SUPER BULKY 6	JUMBO 7
Type of Yarns in Category	Fingering, size 10 crochet thread	Sock, Fingering, Baby	Sport, Baby	DK, Light Worsted	Worsted, Afghan, Aran	Chunky, Craft, Rug	Super Bulky, Roving	Jumbo, Roving
Knit Gauge Ranges in Stockinette St to 4" (10 cm)	33-40 sts**	27-32 sts	23-26 sts	21-24 sts	16-20 sts	12-15 sts	7-11 sts	6 sts and fewer
Advised Needle Size Range	000 to 1	1 to 3	3 to 5	5 to 7	7 to 9	9 to11	11 to 17	17 and larger

* GUIDELINES ONLY: The chart above reflects the most commonly used gauges and needle sizes for specific yarn categories.

** Lace weight yarns are usually knitted on larger needles to create lacy openwork patterns. Accordingly, a gauge range is difficult to determine. Always follow the gauge stated in your pattern.

E-WRAP CAST ON

Make a loop with the working yarn *(Fig. 1)* and place it on the right hand needle; repeat for number of stitches required.

Fig. 1

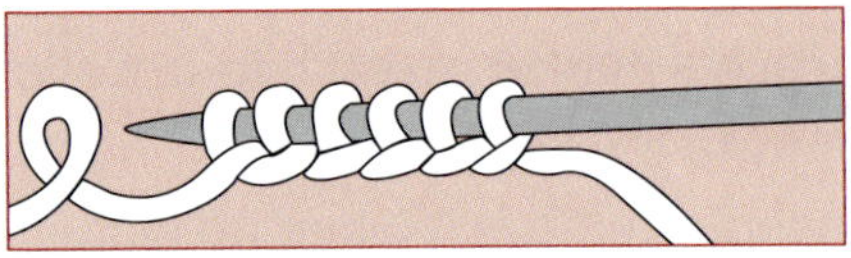

USING A CIRCULAR NEEDLE

Cast on as many stitches as instructed. Untwist and straighten the stitches on the needle to be sure that the cast on ridge lays on the inside of the needle and never rolls around the needle.

Hold the needle so that the ball of yarn is attached to the stitch closest to the right hand point. Working each round on the outside of the the circle with the **right** side of the knitting facing you, work across the stitches on the left hand point *(Fig. 2)*.

Check to be sure that the cast on edge has not twisted around the needle. If it has, it is impossible to untwist it. The only way to fix this is to rip it out and return to the cast on row.

Fig. 2

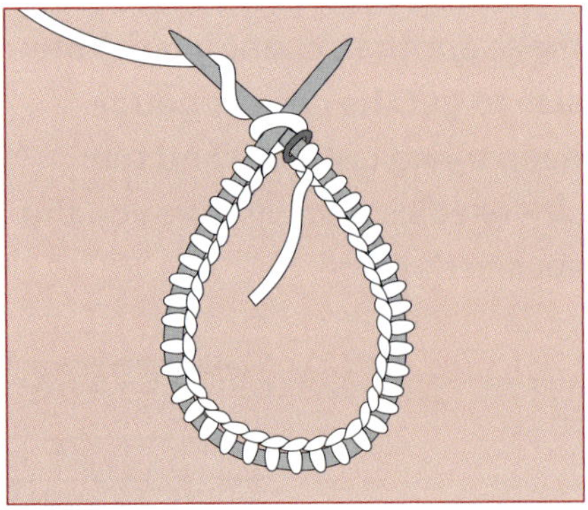

USING DOUBLE POINTED NEEDLES

Cast on as many stitches as instructed. Divide the stitches evenly onto three double pointed needles ***(Fig. 3a)***. Form a triangle with the needles ***(Fig. 3b)***.
Do **not** twist the cast on ridge.

With the remaining needle, work across the stitches on the first needle. You will now have an empty needle with which to work the stitches from the next needle. Work the first stitch of each needle firmly to prevent gaps. Continue working around without turning the work.

Fig. 3a

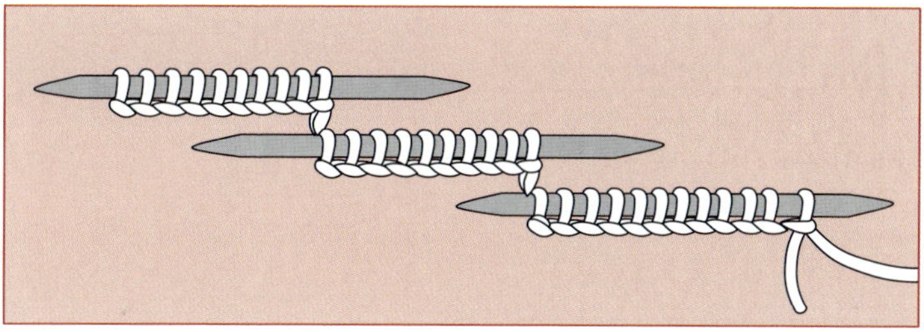

Fig. 3b

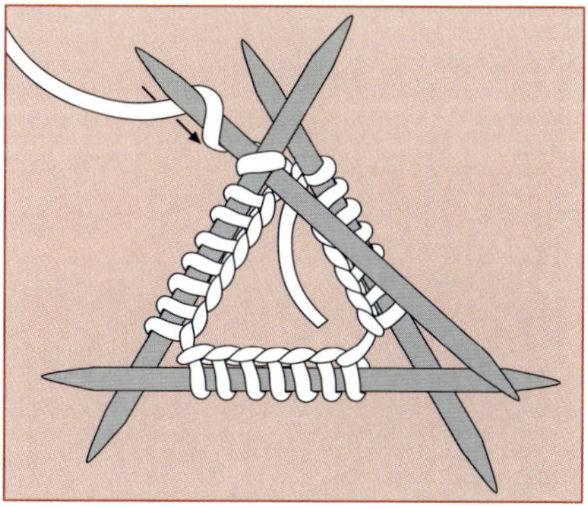

SLIP, SLIP, KNIT

(abbreviated SSK)

Separately slip two stitches as if to **knit** *(Fig. 4a)*. Insert the left needle into the **front** of both slipped stitches *(Fig. 4b)* and **knit** them together as if they were one stitch *(Fig. 4c)*.

Fig. 4a

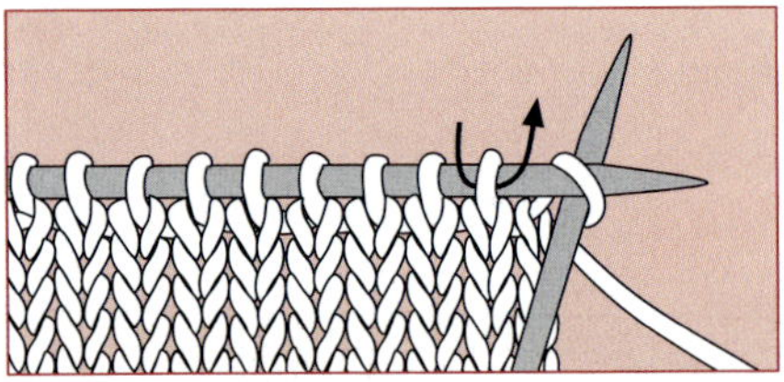

Fig. 4b

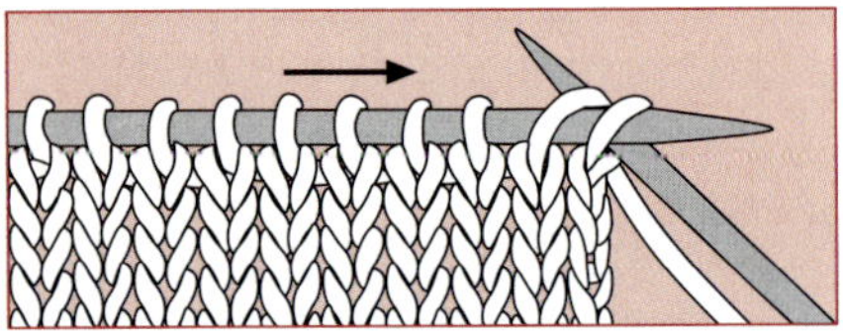

Fig. 4c

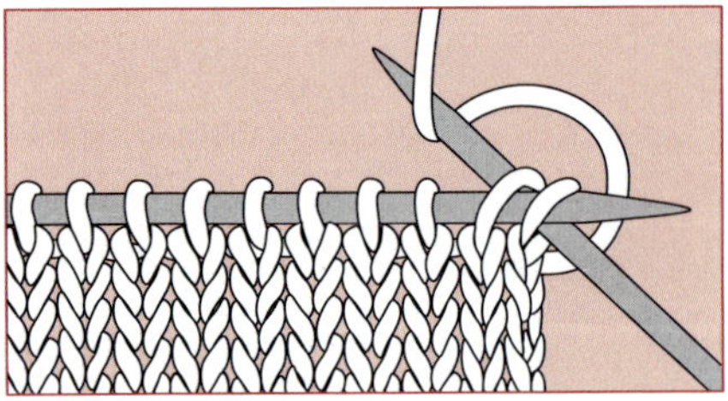

PURL 2 TOGETHER

(abbreviated P2 tog)

Insert the right needle into the **front** of the first two stitches on the left needle as if to **purl** *(Fig. 5)*, then **purl** them together as if they were one stitch.

Fig. 5

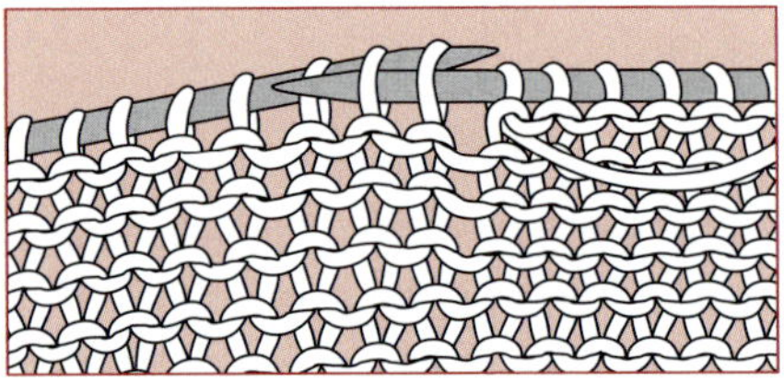

POM-POM

Cut a piece of cardboard 3" (7.5 cm) wide and as long as you want the diameter of your finished pom-pom to be. Wind the yarn around the cardboard until it is your desired thickness in the middle *(Fig. 6a)*.

Carefully slip the yarn off the cardboard and firmly tie an 18" (45.5 cm) length of yarn around the middle *(Fig. 6b)*. Leave yarn ends long enough to attach the pom-pom. Cut the loops on both ends and trim the pom-pom into a smooth ball *(Fig. 6c)*.

To make multi-colored pom-poms, hold together one strand of each color to wind around the cardboard. For a half and half pom-pom, wind one color on one side of the width of the cardboard, then wind the second color on the rest of the width before slipping both colors of yarn off the cardboard.

Fig. 6a

Fig. 6b

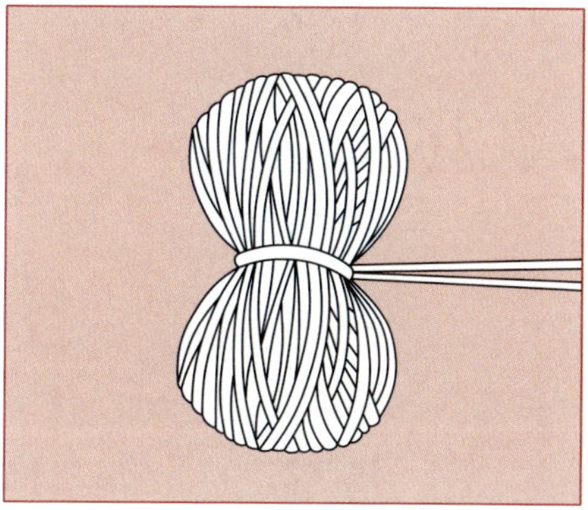

Fig. 6c

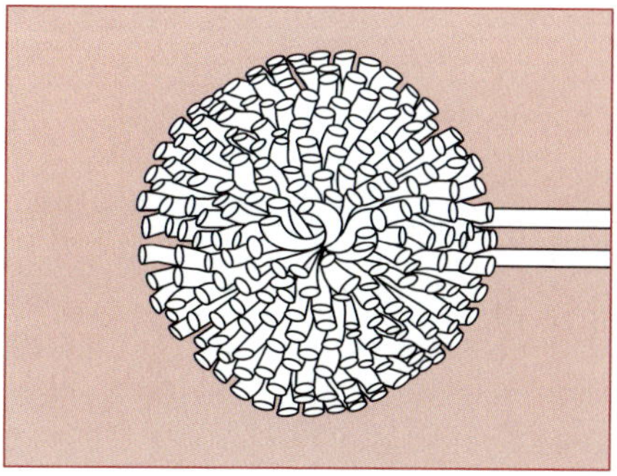

FRINGE

Cut the length of fringe indicated in the individual instructions. Hold together as many strands as indicated in the individual instructions; fold in half.

With the **wrong** side facing and using a crochet hook, draw the folded loop up through both stitches and pull the loose ends through the folded end ***(Fig. 7a)***; draw the knot up **tightly** ***(Fig. 7b)***. Repeat as instructed.

Fig. 7a

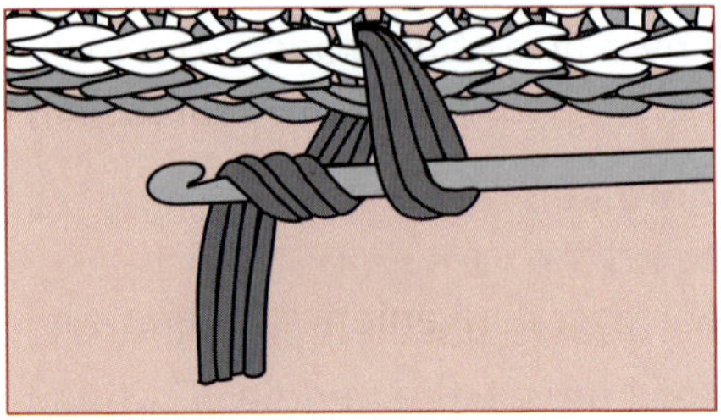

Fig. 7b

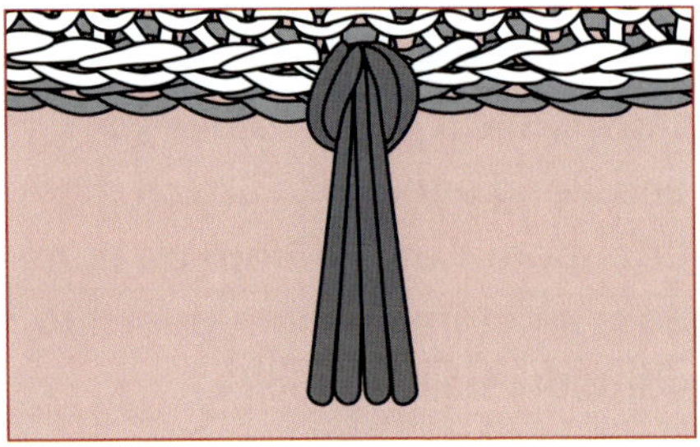

YARN INFORMATION

The cowls in this book were made using various weights of yarn. Any brand of the specified weight of yarn may be used. It is best to refer to the yardage/meters when determining how many balls or skeins to purchase. Remember, to arrive at the finished size, it is the GAUGE/TENSION that is important, not the brand of yarn.
For your convenience, listed below are the specific yarns used to create our photography models. Because yarn manufacturers make frequent changes in their product lines, you may sometimes find it necessary to use a substitute yarn or to search for the discontinued product at alternate suppliers (locally or online).

BOW COWL
Bernat® Mega Bulky™
#88046 Light Grey Heather

FRINGE POCKET COWL
Patons® Classic Wool Bulky™
#89310 Aster Purple

DRAMATIC POM-POM COWL
Lion Brand® Hometown USA®
Pink - #400 Neon Pink
Blue - #105 Detroit Blue
Orange - #133 Syracuse Orange
Purple - #147 Minneapolis Purple
Green - #194 Monterey Lime

FAIR ISLE COWL
Bernat® Wool-Up Bulky™
Orange - #50630 Pumpkin
Cream - #50008 Aran

GARTER FLAP COWL
Lion Brand® Country®
#223 Hampton Sunset

GARTER FRINGE COWL
Version A
Red Heart® Super Saver®
Green - #0672 Spring Green
Variegated - #0964 Primary
Version B
Red Heart® With Love®
Black - #1012 Black
Maroon - #1907 Boysenberry

HERRINGBONE COWL
Lion Brand® Hometown USA®
#107 Charlotte Blue

LOOP STITCH COWL
Red Heart® Stellar™
#9941 Infinity

POM-POM CLOSURE COWL
Red Heart® Boutique Treasure™
#1919 Watercolors

MULTIDIRECTIONAL COWL
Patons® Classic Wool Roving™
Red - #77709 Cherry
Red Heart® Boutique Unforgettable®
Variegated - #3955 Winery

SIDE BUTTONED COWL
Patons® Classic Wool Roving™
Teal - #77203 Pacific Teal
Patons® Colorwul™
Variegated - #90742 Ocean

STRIPED COWL
Bernat® Roving™
Teal - #00203 Teal
Gold - #00609 Squashed

We have made every effort to ensure that these instructions are accurate and complete. We cannot, however, be responsible for human error, typographical mistakes, or variations in individual work.

Production Team: Writer/Instructional Editor - Sarah J. Green; Editorial Writer - Susan Frantz Wiles; Senior Graphic Artist - Lora Puls; Graphic Artist - Frances Huddleston; Photo Stylist - Lori Wenger; and Photographer - Jason Masters.